Badgers

by Derek Zobel

BELLWETHER MEDIA · MINNEAPOLIS, MN

Note to Librarians, Teachers, and Parents:

Blastoff! Readers are carefully developed by literacy experts and combine standards-based content with developmentally appropriate text.

Level 1 provides the most support through repetition of high-frequency words, light text, predictable sentence patterns, and strong visual support.

Level 2 offers early readers a bit more challenge through varied simple sentences, increased text load, and less repetition of high-frequency words.

Level 3 advances early-fluent readers toward fluency through increased text and concept load, less reliance on visuals, longer sentences, and more literary language.

Level 4 builds reading stamina by providing more text per page, increased use of punctuation, greater variation in sentence patterns, and increasingly challenging vocabulary.

Level 5 encourages children to move from "learning to read" to "reading to learn" by providing even more text, varied writing styles, and less familiar topics.

Whichever book is right for your reader, Blastoff! Readers are the perfect books to build confidence and encourage a love of reading that will last a lifetime!

This edition first published in 2012 by Bellwether Media, Inc.

No part of this publication may be reproduced in whole or in part without written permission of the publisher. For information regarding permission, write to Bellwether Media, Inc., Attention: Permissions Department, 5357 Penn Avenue South, Minneapolis, MN 55419.

Library of Congress Cataloging-in-Publication Data
Zobel, Derek, 1983-
  Badgers / by Derek Zobel.
    p. cm. – (Blastoff! readers. Backyard wildlife)
  Includes bibliographical references and index.
  Summary: "Developed by literacy experts for students in kindergarten through grade three, this book introduces badgers to young readers through leveled text and related photos"–Provided by publisher.
  ISBN 978-1-60014-595-7 (hardcover : alk. paper)
  1. Badgers–Juvenile literature. I. Title.
QL737.C25Z63 2012
599.76'7–dc22   2011002250

Printed in the United States of America, North Mankato, MN.

080111   1187

Contents

What Are Badgers?   4

Setts   12

Hunting   16

Staying Safe   18

Glossary   22

To Learn More   23

Index   24

Badgers are **stocky** animals. Their faces are black and white.

Male badgers
are called boars.
Females are
called sows.

Badgers have long, sharp **claws** on their feet. Each foot has five claws.

claws

Badgers use their front feet to dig. Their back feet push the dirt away.

Badgers dig homes in grasslands. Their homes are called **setts**.

Badgers must move often to find food. They dig new setts every few days.

Badgers eat **insects**, gophers, and other small animals. They hunt for **prey** at night.

Other animals hunt badgers. Badgers have tough skin and thick fur to keep them safe.

Badgers dig small holes to stay safe. They back into them, growl, and show their teeth. Keep out!

Glossary

claws—sharp, curved nails on the feet of some animals; claws help badgers dig.

insects—small animals with six legs and hard outer bodies; insect bodies are divided into three parts.

prey—animals that are hunted by other animals for food

setts—badger homes; badgers dig into the ground to make setts.

stocky—short and thick

To Learn More

AT THE LIBRARY

Hoban, Russell. *Bedtime for Frances*. New York, N.Y.: HarperCollins Publishers, 1995.

Howard, Fran. *Badgers: Active at Night*. Mankato, Minn.: Bridgestone Books, 2005.

Leach, Michael. *Badger*. New York, N.Y.: Rosen Pub. Group's PowerKids Press, 2009.

ON THE WEB

Learning more about badgers is as easy as 1, 2, 3.

1. Go to www.factsurfer.com.

2. Enter "badgers" into the search box.

3. Click the "Surf" button and you will see a list of related Web sites.

With factsurfer.com, finding more information is just a click away.

Index

boars, 6
claws, 8
days, 14
dig, 10, 12, 14, 20
faces, 4
feet, 8, 10
food, 14
fur, 18
gophers, 16
grasslands, 12
growl, 20
holes, 20
homes, 12
hunt, 16, 18
insects, 16
night, 16

prey, 16
setts, 12, 14
skin, 18
sows, 6
stocky, 4
teeth, 20